Dominate Upwork - Tips, hacks and strategies to increase your monthly income on the world's biggest freelancing platform

By James Oliver

Contents

Dominate Upwork - Tips, hacks and strategies to increase your monthly income on the world's biggest freelancing platform

    By James Oliver

Contents

Introduction to Freelancing

Foundations for Upwork Success

    Common Upwork/Freelancing Myth - Believing you don't have any skills

Profile

    How to write a captivating profile that stands out from the crowd

    Profile template that you can use regardless of profession

    Actual profile example that got a job invite within the first week

    Your Upwork job title

    Social proof - how to use testimonials

    Smile your way to success

    Profile Tests

    The secret bonus of being Top Rated that Upwork doesn't tell you about

Searching for Jobs

    Job Filters

    The 4 biggest proposal mistakes that 90% of Upworkers make

- Advanced Tips for proposals and bidding on jobs
- How to spot a bad client
- Sample bad proposals
- Sample winning proposal

Client Retention
- How to retain over half your clients
- Your rates and how to raise them

Summary

Introduction to Freelancing

Freelancing is one of the easiest online businesses to break into. Unlike dropshipping, affiliate marketing or any other online work, you can make money from day 1 without spending a single penny on inventory or months building up an email list.

Upwork is currently the biggest online freelancing marketplace in the world. Every day over 10,000 jobs are posted on the site. Those jobs collectively pay millions to those who win the contracts.

But with over 12 million freelancers signed up, competition is fierce. That's why I'm going to show you the competitive edges you need to win these jobs, increase your hourly rates and make a full-time living freelancing on Upwork.

I've been on Upwork for over 4 years (back when it was eLance and oDesk) as both a client and a freelancer. I've bid and won countless jobs and have enough repeat business and private job invites where I rarely have to apply to public jobs any more.

But don't worry - I started out just like you.

My profile was full of mistakes, I would bid on 30 jobs and win none of them, and I never received a single job invite in my first 2 years on the site.

In this book I am going to lay out the steps that I took to go from making $54 a month to making enough money to quit my corporate job and live full time off my Upwork earnings. If you apply them, you will make more money.

You'll learn

- How I get 50-100x more profile views than the average Upwork freelancer
- How to write proposals to get you chosen ahead of 50 other candidates
- How to spot bad clients and avoid wasting your time bidding on their jobs
- How I turned a $220 job into $9,000 worth of work

...and much, much more

Foundations for Upwork Success

Before diving into the steps needed to succeed on Upwork, we should take some time to cover the fundamental approaches and tactics you need to be aware of when working on the platform.

The Golden Rule: Freelancing on Upwork is a business.

There's no two ways about it, if you are an Upwork freelancer, you are in control of your own business, your reputation and your client base.

Even if your Upwork earnings aren't your main income source yet, you should treat your clients like they are. A lot of people believe that the online nature of Upwork is an excuse to avoid common courtesy. This applies to clients as well as freelancers.

As a freelancer two of the most important things you can do are respond promptly to messages and deliver work on time. This alone will put you in the top half of Upwork users. Upwork may have a huge user base, but due to the low barriers to entry needed to sign up, a large portion of these users are very low quality and can't even follow these simple guidelines.

For example, if you search freelancers by the skill "writing", there are over 920,000 results. But, 70% of these freelancers haven't won a single job, and less than 3% have lifetime earnings of over $10,000. This goes to show that you are overestimating the quality of your competition, and by taking the steps in this guide you can put yourself in that 3%.

A specialist in a world of generalists - The importance of having a niche

If you've ever watched Kitchen Nightmares with Gordon Ramsey - you'll know that often the biggest problem with the restaurants is that the menu is too big, and thus all of the food on offer is very average. It's extremely difficult to cook 50 or 100 items well.

The same principle applies in freelancing, it's difficult to do 10 or 15 different jobs to a high standard. Which is why you should concentrate on just 1 or 2 areas of expertise.

The following areas are a race to the bottom and you will be forced to compete on price, no matter what. It is hard to earn anything more than $12-15/h in these fields

- Admin support
- Virtual assistance
- Customer service
- Cold calling

The good news is, It's possible to earn a full time living on Upwork in so many other areas. Everything from blog writing to UX design to accountancy can be lucrative if you position yourself correctly.

Another benefit of having a niche is that you only need a few good clients to provide you with enough work. Take it from experience when I say it is infinitely easier to work on 2 or 3 projects at once than it is to work on 6 or 7.

Finding your niche takes time, and if you're just starting out then you may be overwhelmed with the options available. But after a few jobs you will start to get an idea of what works and what doesn't.

If you have no idea where to start - one way of seeing what jobs are in demand is just to browse the Upwork job boards every day. There may be fads that pop up (e.g. in June/July 2016 when Pokemon Go related content was huge) or you just start to notice services that people need year round.

Common Upwork/Freelancing Myth - Believing you don't have any skills

Yes you do, you just don't realise it.

Thanks to the internet, the vast majority of freelancing skills can be learned.

You don't need a computer science degree to charge $5,000+ for a website

You don't need a copywriting degree (do these even exist?) to charge $100/h

You don't need to have graduated in video production or have 10 years industry experience to make a full time living freelancing in that area

Will you make these figures straight away? No, probably not.

Is it completely conceivable to make good money doing these things with less than 2 years of experience? Absolutely.

I had never written a blog post before someone paid me to write one. Do you know how I knew how to do it? I literally Googled "How to write a blog post".

I already knew the basic structure form reading blogs and with my 5 minutes of Google knowledge I was fully prepared to write one.

Was it the best blog post ever? Nope.

Did I get paid for it? Sure I did.

You are very rarely good at anything the first time, but guess what? You are better the second time round, and the third and so on.

My $100 blog posts weren't that different from my $10 blog posts, just minor improvements that allowed me to charge a higher price.

There has never been so much free information out there. You can know learn to write, code, design and a ton of other skills by spending little to no money.

Another common complaint from failing Upworkers is that you can't make money if you're not a native English speaker. This is total BS - do you know how many freelance translation jobs there are out there? Or SEO in languages other than English.

Just think outside the box a little and suddenly the possibilities increase tenfold.

If you feel more comfortable with some sort of formal qualifications or certification. There are tons of online courses that you can take will provide you both with education in a certain field, some will even give you a qualification at the end of it. As a bonus, adding online certifications is a great way to bolster your public profile.

Online course resources:

Hubspot.com - marketing - 5 free in-depth courses

Udemy.com - multiple fields - paid courses ranging from $30 to $500+, they often have sales discounting courses by up to 90%

Freecodecamp.com - Programming languages/web development - free

Alison.com - multiple fields - free

Profile

Your profile is your gateway to job invites. It's your chance to sell yourself and stand out in a sea of average freelancers. It's also how you are going to be found in Upwork's search engine and how you get recommended for public jobs that people post.

My profile gets around 80-100 views per month, the Upwork average is 1-2. Now imagine yourself at 50 views per month, even at a 10% conversion rate that's still more than 1 targeted job invite per week. Once your profile is on point, you will save huge amounts of time by not having to search for public jobs on Upwork's job boards.

The profile problem is simple - too many people look at their profile like a resume

All they do talk about themselves and how great they are at their particular job. This sounds logical right?

Wrong. Dead wrong.

Clients don't care about your masters degree (or lack of one), or your 7 years of corporate experience. All they care about is what you can do for them.

So let's flip the problem around. Who is your ideal client? What does your client want from you? What do you provide that other freelancers don't? You need to look at your profile from you client's point of view.

Let's take a look at a typical low quality public profile. This is one I took directly from Upwork, in the copywriting niche.

"I have over 10 years of experience as a copywriter. This includes writing all kinds of copy including Webinars, Video Sales Letters, Sales Letters, Emails, Headlines, Titles, Ads, Etc. Please see the project examples in my portfolio that I created. I look forward to answering any additional questions you may have and discussing your specific needs."

Let's start with the first sentence, the most important one of all.

"I have over 10 years of experience as a copywriter."

That's nice in the corporate world, but this is Upwork. The client is already thinking "so what?" What is their incentive for reading on here?

Let's keep going

"This includes writing all kinds of copy including Webinars, Video Sales Letters, Sales Letters, Emails, Headlines, Titles, Ads, Etc. Please see the project examples in my portfolio that I created."

Not bad - but what results have they achieved with any of these. Also when listings the various types of work you do, do it in bullet points. It reads a lot better this way.

"I look forward to answering any additional questions you may have and discussing your specific needs."

There is no call to action here. What if a client wants to get in contact with you - where do they go? What buttons should they click? You may have lost a potential sale by not directing them.

This profile doesn't address any potential client needs, has no call to action and only talks about the freelancer.

How to write a captivating profile that stands out from the crowd

Use this easy 5-step profile checklist:

1. Does your first sentence encourage a client to keep reading?
2. Do you address your potential client's needs/wants/desires?
3. Do you show that your previous work has achieved results?
4. Have you included keywords that clients are likely to search for?
5. Have you included a call-to-action at the end to get the client to take the next step?

As long as you cover these 5 steps, your profile is already better than a large portion of your competition. Keep your ideal client in mind while writing it to avoid getting caught in the "me me me" trap that many profiles suffer from.

To make it even easier for yourself. Write out on a piece of paper your client's buyer search persona. This is a fictional persona that is used by marketers to create a picture of your ideal customer, or in the case of Upwork, your ideal client. This includes how they will search for you on the platform. Here are some questions you can use

- What is the size of their business?
- What do they want to accomplish from your service?
- What is their biggest challenge that you will solve? Be as specific as possible with this one

- What language will they use in their searches?

Let's create a fictional buyer persona for a small business that needs a web designer.

Why do they need a web designer?

This could be as simple as someone told them that they need an online presence to grow their business. There's no harm in re-iterating this.

Why would they hire someone to do this?

If they're a small business, it's probably the owner/founder doing the searching. You will save them time. Time that as a small business owner, they don't have a lot of. People want to spend time working on their business, not in their business. The other big reason is that they probably don't have the necessary web design skills.

What are their goals from your service?

Inform customers about their offering, grow their email lists, increase subscribers and expand their customer reach.

If you've already done jobs in this area, you can talk about results you've achieved from previous clients. Always use numbers instead of vague terms like "good performance" where possible.

What language will they use in their searches?

Will they search for web design or web designer? - Small tweaks to your profile overview and title like this one make a huge difference.

Profile template that you can use regardless of profession

This template is designed for newbies or people who need a complete profile overhaul. Once you find your Upwork area of specialty then you can add extra details to help your cause.

"Do you want to <common client goal?>

If you want to accomplish <client goal> then you need to do/have <something related to the service you provide>

<Accomplishing client goal> will bring you <tangible results>

I can help you do that by <explain what you do>

List your specialties in bullet point form (this is great for listing multiple keywords)

If you're still reading this, we're probably about to be best friends. If you're looking for <skill> your customers benefit from, click the green "Contact" button on the top of the page"

Actual profile example that got a job invite within the first week

"Having compelling web content is invaluable if you want to drive traffic to your website and convert leads into customers.

Do you feel like you have a great product or service but can't convey that to your target audience?

Maybe you need help with creating copy for your website and don't know where to start.

Or you have existing web content that you need updating to appeal to a modern market.

Then you need someone to step in and take this stuff off your hands so that you can concentrate on the big picture.

If you're looking for:

- Blog posts that your readers share on social media and get found in Google searches

- Landing page copy that converts potential leads into email subscribers

- About pages that tell your customers the unique story behind your business - this is usually the second most visited page on your site!

- Facebook/Instagram ads that bring you paying customers via social media

- Email campaigns that your readers open and respond to, even if you don't have an email list yet!

- Video scripts that bring your explainer or whiteboard videos to life

- Keyword research to help you become more visible on Google and other search engines (SEO)

- Consultation and feedback on PPC/AdWords campaigns - no more wasting money on irrelevant leads

Then I can help you.

Chances are, you didn't get into business to spend all day writing blog posts or working on an inbound content marketing strategy.

You got into business to help people and make money doing something you enjoy.

I want to give you more time to work on your business, not in your business.

If it sounds like we'd be a good fit, then hit one of those buttons in the top right area of this page and let's get to know each other."

Your Upwork job title

Your job title is the first thing that people will see next to your name - and it's vital you have a good one.

Too many freelancers take the job title too literally and just state what they do

"Accountant"

"Tax Attorney"

"Content writer"

"Marketing Expert"

That's why you see hundreds of people with the exact same title.

Your new approach should be to feature a client benefit in your title - you get to use 70 characters so use your space wisely. Here are some examples of great Upwork titles

"Story-Based Copywriter Who Gets Emotional Response & High Conversions"

"Graphic Design that generates revenue for Small Businesses"

"Your Conversion-Obsessed Sales Writer."

"Squarespace Website Design & Minimalist Web Design"

"Experience Design to Enhance your Startup | Web | UX/UI | Branding"

"Experienced CPA and CFO for Amazon FBA and Shopify Sellers"

Don't be afraid to use extra keywords in your title as well. This will help you get discovered in search engines.

Social proof - how to use testimonials

One of the main advantages of Upwork as a platform is that clients can see your reviews from previous jobs.

Why do you think sites like Amazon feature customer reviews so heavily? Because we buy things that our peers like.

Think about it - when was the last time you bought a product online without looking at reviews?

Upwork is the same, your client reviews are so important. If you're good at what you do, your clients probably have all kinds of nice things to say about you.

You can use these reviews to your advantage in more ways than one.

So copy and paste them from the feedback section and put them in your profile overview. Inserting them right at the top of your overview is ideal but you can also sprinkle them in here and there.

It doesn't matter how big the job was - I personally used a testimonial I got from a $5 job for over 9 months because the client left a really great, detailed review.

The more specific the review is, the better - for example "Built me a fast, mobile optimized ecommerce site" is better than "Good web designer"

Any reviews were the client mentions your results are the best, but if you don't have them - ones that say you did a great job are fine too.

If you don't have any Upwork reviews yet. Apply to jobs that offer 5 star feedback in exchange for work. These don't pay well at all but are worth it just to get 1 or 2 initial reviews.

Smile your way to success

Your picture is the first thing that a client's eye is drawn to. It's the ultimate first impression on Upwork. It's very easy to both win and lose jobs just from your profile picture.

Luckily there's only one thing you really need to do - **SMILE**

It's proven that people who smile are seen as more likable and trustworthy. And put on some nice clothes, a suit makes you look professional and qualified.

No selfies or weird photo filters either. Just get a friend to take the photo.

Your profile length

You'll see online that a lot of people advise keeping your Upwork profile as short as possible. Even Upwork themselves encourage this. However, I disagree with this idea. Long profiles are only bad if they're boring. If you keep a client engaged then by all means use a longer profile. If you're going to charge $75/h+, then you'll probably need to write more than just a few sentences.

Here's a snippet from a fantastic long Upwork profile to prove my point

"But I can assure you, I am indeed the Ultra Persuasive Sales Sith Lord I make myself out to be...

And I'll prove it to you.

How?

Well, you just read 787 words of an online profile of a person you didn't even know existed 5 minutes ago."

(This person charges $125/h by the way)

Creating scarcity

If you are getting to the point where you have more than enough work to stay busy, talk about this in your profile. If you let clients know that you are so in demand that you rarely take on new work, then you appear even more desirable. In turn, this allows you to charge even higher rates.

You can also specify the kind of clients you want, and don't want to work with. If you're uncomfortable designing adult websites or writing copy for pick up artists then state that. Once again, only do this if you are busy enough and can afford to miss out on the potential work.

Location Specifics

If you are a native English speaker living abroad - set your location as your home nation. This especially applies to location independent workers and digital nomads who live outside of their place of birth.

This will allow you to not be excluded when clients search for freelancers by North America/Europe etc.

E.G. If you are a US citizen living in Thailand, leave your location as your US home town. This is so you still appear in searches for freelancers based in North America. These searches are designed to filter out non-native speakers, not expats.

You can explain to clients that you are based in another client when discussing the project - and 99% of them won't care.

Profile Tests

Upwork tests are important - but not for the reasons you think

Upwork clients don't care about your test scores, but the Upwork search engine does.

There is one test that absolutely every freelancer should take - The Upwork freelancer readiness test.

This particular test features a few questions about the Upwork platform and freelancing in general. Unlike the other tests, this one literally takes less than 5 minutes and the answers are obvious to anyone with a fifth grade education.

Score 100% and slap it on your profile for a boost in rankings! Those who have this score on their profile always rank higher than an equivalent profile that doesn't.

Recommended tests:

Any test relevant to your niche - spelling, grammar, technical tests. Once again, these affect your rankings.

For technical tests for areas like web development, video editing, accounting etc. - These are vital to your rankings. If clients select certain skills when posting a job and you have scored in the top 20% for a test. Then your profile will be given preference over others.

The secret bonus of being Top Rated that Upwork doesn't tell you about

You can't please everyone all the time. Occasionally you are going to run into a client who gives you less than 5 star feedback. However, Upwork has a way to counter this that they DON'T OPENLY ADVERTISE.

If you are a Top Rated Freelancer - you can remove 1 piece of bad feedback per month from your profile and increase your job success score. It's unlikely that you'll need to use this every month, but it does come in handy when you do need it.

The following is buried deep in the Upwork help section.

Removing a contract's feedback to exercise more control over your Job Success Score (JSS) is one of the perks of the Top Rated program. Top Rated freelancers and agencies have earned this perk through consistently excellent delivery to their clients.

As a Top Rated freelancer, you can request to remove one job on Upwork's feedback from your Job Success Score. You can also choose whether to remove the client's public rating and comment (if any) from your profile.

How to request feedback removal for a contract:

First find the contract number - To do this go to your contracts page. Find the contract you'd like to remove and click on it. On the right-hand side of the page, in the Contract Details section, you will find the Contract ID.

Email freelancersuccess@upwork.com and provide the contract number that you would like to have removed.

The request will be processed within 7 days. Any impact on your JSS would appear the next time your score updates after the removal is processed.

Searching for Jobs

Your main aim as an Upwork freelancer should be to get as many job invites as possible. However the public job boards can still be a source of great clients.

Job Filters

Many online blogs will advise setting up tons of filters to "weed out bad clients", I disagree with this approach. Just because a client is new, doesn't make them bad. The same goes for filtering entry level/intermediate/expert positions. Let me tell you that very few clients pay attention to this while posting a job, and many clients will select entry level as Upwork suggests that's where they will pay the lowest rates.

Client budget for fixed rate jobs is also in the same boat here. How many times have you seen a complex job posted with a $5 budget, way too many right? But the client doesn't honestly expect to pay just $5 for this, most of the time they won't have any clue what they should be paying and will expect the freelancer to give them a cost estimate.

The point here is, the Upwork job board is a smorgasbord of potential clients, so don't limit yourself. Setting one or two filters is OK but excess filters will mean you miss out on some great jobs.

Don't be afraid to look through other categories either, it's not uncommon for a client to post a job in the wrong one.

Proposals

With a limited amount of proposals (30 per month, or 1 per day) - it's vital that you learn how to write a good one.

When I started on Upwork, one of the most disheartening scenes was clicking on a good looking job post and seeing that 20-50 people had already applied. I'd click straight out of the window and continue looking.

On the flip side - I've also posted jobs as a client that received 50+ invitations and I still had to go elsewhere to hire someone because every single proposal was, in a word, awful.

What I didn't realize at the time was one simple thing - I was overestimating my competition. The majority of these proposals are just not very good. Either single job post receives a ton of generic copy and pasted messages from people who want to win a job, not that job.

I once posted a job that got 56 proposals. The job was fairly straightforward and only included 2 screening questions. Do you know how many people answered both screening questions properly and sent me a sample of their work?

Zero.

Zip.

Nada.

Not even one out of 56 bothered to read the proposal through and show me they could help me with my needs. Some of these people were trying to charge $100/h as well, which goes to show that the rate on someone's profile isn't always indicative of their abilities.

I've hired less qualified people for jobs because they showed me a good sample and demonstrated to me in their proposal that they understood my needs. It's not rocket science, it's human connection.

The better your proposals, the easier it is to win jobs. Easy wins build momentum and confidence - back when I was charging $2/100 words I could never have imagined that I could regularly win jobs that paid $50/100 words. But after a few jobs you start to believe in yourself more, which is vital in freelancing success.

The 4 biggest proposal mistakes that 90% of Upworkers make

1. They use a stock cover letter

This is the easiest way to get rejected for a job. Every single proposal you write should be targeted at the job itself. Not only are generic "copy and paste" proposals very easy to spot (believe me, I've seen a lot), but they're also widely ineffective.

It takes a lot less time than you think to write a good, focused proposal. Most of the proposals I write take me less than 15 minutes, and that includes researching the client and the job,

2. They only talk about themselves

How many times have you started a proposal with "I would be a good fit for this job because…"

Too often people only talk about their skills or qualifications, they fail to mention the client's needs at all. Much like your profile, try to make your proposals as client-focused as possible.

Try using sentences like these

- I see you are looking for <skillset>
- I would be able to help you/your project
- To accomplish your goals you require <task>

Research the client, if they've provided a link to their website, go on it and see if you can use anything on there as leverage. Even 5 or 10 minutes of research can help you write a great client-focused proposal.

If the opportunity arises, give the client a compliment. For example if they have a really cool product or website design, tell them that - they'd love to hear it.

3. They don't show relevant work samples

Samples are the lifeblood of proposals. It's tough to get hired without them. But here is where people overthink things.

You don't need to have a huge portfolio of work. For almost every job I apply for now I use the same 3 or 4 samples of work, because they are all relevant and high performing. It also helps that most of the jobs I apply for are for the exact same task.

But where a lot of people make a mistake is showing an irrelevant sample, or no sample at all. If a client needs a blog post about healthcare, you showing them a sales letter doesn't demonstrate that you can do the job. It's like if someone wants me to tailor a shirt and I show them a pair of shoes that I fixed. Yes it's in the same vague category of work, but your samples should be as specific as possible.

If you don't have samples, make one up on the spot. If someone's job is looking for someone to write blog posts about the best Mexican food in NYC, write a few hundred words about the best sushi in Houston. The sample is relevant without just giving the client free work.

Your sample should never actually be targeted at the job itself, don't gave free work away to clients. It loses you money, and it's against Upwork's terms of service. In the how to spot bad clients section, I cover this in more detail.

4. They don't use a call-to-action

Every piece of communication you send should have a call to action (CTA). This can be as simple as asking a question about the job or inquiring if the client can discuss the project over Skype for 10 minutes. Nothing major, just give them one focused decision to make.

Try to stay away from vague CTAs that require excess thought - thought leads to inaction. How often do you hear the phrase "I can't decide what to wear?" - because there are just too many options. If you have 1 pair of jeans and 1 t-shirt, then guess what you're wearing each day?

With regards to clients, send them very closed questions with only 1 possible answer. This was you to can continue the conversation and then lead them down the path to closing a sale.

Phrases like "looking forward to hearing from you" or even worse "looking forward to working with you" are assumptive, and give off the wrong impression. If you push too hard early on, then the client is likely to pull back and not want to work with you on the job. On the other hand, if you take the soft and slow approach, you will eventually start closing them without even having to sell your services at all. Proposals should be used to start a conversation, not end one.

Finding common ground

Freelancing is a people business and people like working with people they like. They would rather hire (and rehire) a good developer/writer/accountant with a great attitude than a great one with a lousy attitude.

If you can find common ground with the client, don't be afraid to use it. For example if you're from the same state/country/town or the client has work that you are genuinely interested in, let them know. People like to work with people, not robots.

Proofreading

Read your proposal out loud, if you stumble over words then it sounds awkward to a reader as well. Re-write until it flows smoothly.

Before you submit a proposal, take a 5 minute break and re-read one more time before submitting to avoid any errors.

Advanced Tips for proposals and bidding on jobs

The Cover Letter Error

The majority of proposals put a ton of effort in the "cover letter" section of the proposal and neglect the additional questions.

What Upwork doesn't tell you as a freelancer, is that these additional questions actually show up first when the client is viewing a proposal. I recommend introducing yourself and putting the most effort into the first additional question as this is what the client will see first when they click on your proposal.

Answering additional questions too literally

If you've bid on a few Upwork jobs, then you'll have noticed that the same additional questions repeat themselves over again. This is because when you post a job, Upwork gives the client a stock list of 15 questions that they can add to their job post. These include

- Have you taken any Upwork tests and done well on them that you think are

relevant to this job?

- Which of the required job skills do you feel you are strongest at?

- Why do you think you are a good fit for this particular project?

Many proposals make the mistake of answering these too literally, which is the logical thing to do. However, that doesn't get the client excited.

Instead you can use these additional questions to showcase your previous success, send a sample of your work or continue to address the client's needs.

Let's use the question "Why do you think you are a good fit for this particular project?"

Logical, uninspiring answer:

I'm good at skill x, skill y and I work in a timely manner with no mistakes etc.

Exciting answer:

<Positive testimonial from previous Upwork client>

Above is a testimonial regarding a job I did for a previous client. This project sounds similar to yours…

I achieved <tangible result>.

As a client that's much more exciting than the logical answer and will put them in a position where they'd love to work with you.

Client Analysis

Check the clients hire rate on their job posting - if it's ridiculously low (<15%) then don't apply, these people just post Upwork jobs to try and get free work or are testing the market to see what they should be paying for a particular service.

I find average hourly rate doesn't have as much of an effect as you'd think. If clients are running a large business they may have a low average hourly rate because they're paying a full-time Filipino virtual assistant $4/h, but they'd still be willing to pay $40/h+ for more skilled work.

How to spot a bad client

Upwork has thousands of great clients, but unfortunately there are a number of bad ones as well. There's a self-destructive mindset that many freelancers have where you believe you have to work with everyone that gives you an opportunity. This couldn't be further from the truth. This is a two-way business and you should do your due diligence to ensure that the client is a good fit for you as well. If you can learn how to spot bad clients, then you can easily avoid wasting your time and proposal connects on them.

Red Flag 1: They don't know what they want

If a client can't tell you want they want from a project, you're going to have a bad time. If there are no clear goals for the project, you will end up nowhere.

If you've been discussing a project with a potential client for a while and you're still no closer to an end goal, just walk away from the communication. It saves you time and their money. The best Upwork clients will always have clear goals for their projects.

Red Flag 2: They demand constant communication

This may sound counter intuitive as communication is always good. But some clients push it too far, if the job description requires you to be "available 24/7" or "always on Skype" then it's likely that you're going to be micro-managed and the client will demand project updates when they don't even need them. As a general rule of thumb, you shouldn't need to communicate with a client more than once or twice per day after the project outlines have been set.

Red Flag 3: They ask for a free "sample"

If a job post asks for a free sample as part of your proposal, then simply move on. Not only if this against Upwork's terms of service, it's also a way for the client to get the entire job done for free. I can't stress this enough - never do free work on Upwork.

Consider this example. A client proposal asks for a sample blog post about your favorite holiday destination. If the job gets 50 proposals and just 10 people send in a sample, the client now has 10 different articles for free.

If you're asked for a sample during the negotiation process, make sure you will be paid for it. More importantly, establish the regular job price before submitting any samples. If you don't, one sample piece at half your regular rate can suddenly become 2 or 3.

Red Flag 4: They need the work done yesterday

It's very rare that a job is truly "urgent" or "needed within 12 hours". If you do sign up for one of these gigs you can expect non-stop hassle and demands throughout the entire project.

On a rare occasion where a client does genuinely need work in a short time frame, increase your price for the job to reflect this.

Red Flag 5: They immediately ask to work off Upwork

Usually this is done via invited jobs, but it happens on public jobs too. You get a message from a client interested in your work, but they want to use a different platform for payment. Common excuses include "it will take 2 weeks for us to set up Upwork payment" or "it will be easier for us to communicate". These clients are likely to scam you into working for free.

Red Flag 6: Bad client rating

Just like a client is unlikely to hire you if your Job Success Score is under 80%, you should avoid working with clients with a rating of less than 3.5 stars. If they have more than a few reviews then there is no reason for anything less than a 4 star rating. This usually reflects poor communication, delayed payments and general unfriendliness.

Copy and paste script you can use to end communication with a bad client

"Hi <client name>,

Thank you so much for the opportunity to explore working on your project together. Regrettably, after some further consideration I've come to realize I'm not the best (your job title) for your particular needs.

Thank you for considering me and I wish you all the best on the project.

Thanks,

<Your name>"

Chinese Clients

As a rule, I don't work with Chinese clients. The reason for this is two-fold. Number one, their business culture is one that focuses too much on price over quality of work. They would rather hire 5 different people for $10 to do a job than one person for $50. They are also culturally ingrained to find something wrong with your work. In the Western world we happily give a 5 star rating for a good job, in China you're looking at 3 or 4 stars for the same work, this can greatly affect your job success score. If you don't believe this little hypothesis, Go to Booking.com and check the average rating from a Chinese hotel guest vs. the average American guest.

Fixed Rate vs. Hourly

For all Upwork projects, you can either work at a fixed rate or an hourly rate. An hourly rate is how much you charge for each hour of work (this is tracked using Upwork software). A fixed price is how much you charge for the whole job, regardless of how many hours it takes.

Hourly work is always guaranteed, meaning you will get paid for any time spent working. Fixed-rate jobs are not guaranteed but Upwork now implements escrow services which means they hold the money until the job is completed. This eliminates the potential problem of the client refusing to pay for work.

You should set your rates to be equal. For example, if your hourly rate is $35 per hour, you should charge $7 per 100 words if it takes you 60 minutes to write 500 words.

I personally prefer working hourly as it ensures you are paid for your time. But once you do certain jobs over and over again, you will get a feeling for how long it will take you and you can set an accurate fixed rate for the project.

If a client is asking you for an estimate on a project and you aren't sure of how long it will take. Increase your estimate by 50%. Trust me when I say that the first time you do a job, it will take longer than expected. There is nothing worse than starting a big project, then realising halfway through that you have drastically undercharged the client. This is very hard to rectify as well, because no one likes being told they will have to spend more money than previously agreed. Your best bet in this situation is just to eat the cost and use it as a lesson learned for the future.

Sample bad proposals

These are a few sample of proposals I have personally received on Upwork. Personal details are removed because this isn't meant to be an attack on the people who submitted them. I just want you to learn from these mistakes.

Job Title: Copywriter Needed For Landing Page Optimization

Proposal from "Marketing Consultant and Copywriter" - $85/h

"Thank you for the opportunity to work with you. Some of my clients have told me that hiring me was the best investment they've ever made. I'm not going to tell you to believe me but see what some of my clients have said:

"As a result of his efforts we had the most sales we've had in any quarter in our history." Tony Smith, USA Today Travel Marketing Division

"<name removed> is a copywriting genius. He was great, thought through the open-ended marketing task that was given to him and came up with highly effective sales copy for our landing page. Definitely don't waste your time taking applications from other providers. The work has been done for you!" Jeffrey Gordon, New Peak

"A top class copywriter. Highly recommended" - Zed Chama, Nine Province

"The sales letter <name removed> wrote for me took what I do to the next letter" - Les Brown, America's top ranked motivational speaker

"I commissioned <name removed> to write copy for me and what he wrote turned into one of the my top selling items" - Bob Bly (McGraw Hill called him "one of America's top copywriters")

As you consider the benefits of hiring me you might like to imagine what a higher conversion rate will mean - consistently more customers and increased profits day after day and month after month for as long as you continue to use what I've written. You may not be aware that how I write copy is unlike most contractors quoting on this job... I use a proven, highly persuasive languaging approach called NLP (neuro-linguistic program) that melts away prospect resistance causing many to buy...."

Do you notice how the first sentence already assumes he's won the job? As a client, that immediately puts me on the back foot and puts me in a state of mind where I don't want to work with him. If we go on further, we're 275 words in and he still hasn't addressed my job. Do you think this inspires me or gets me excited to work with him, despite his obvious credentials? Absolutely not.

Here's another one for the same job

Proposal from: "Creator of powerful, high converting copy" - $155/h

"hi there

I would like to help you with this project.

Here's how I differ to other copywriters on here...

It's in the results I deliver.

Check out the amazing conversions in this video:

3.29% to cold traffic from a previous 1% after I re-wrote the copy

<youtube video>

A recent client of mine made $60k in 7 days with his copy.

His video testimonial is here along with many others.

<link to webpage>

Another client made $125k in 4 days with his copy.

His testimonial is on the same page

Work samples are here

<link to samples> "

No personal introduction, no addressing the needs of my job. Just talking about how great he is. He doesn't mention landing pages, nor did he address the additional questions I posted in any detail.

With both of these proposals, the freelancers were charging huge money, but neither could take the time to write a personalized proposal. Once again, this shows that a well researched high quality proposal always trumps previous job experience or paper credentials.

Sample winning proposal

Now here's the winning proposal for that same job

What questions do you have about the project?

Can you share the existing landing page with me? What's your current conversion rate? How are you driving traffic to the site? I'll have more specific questions once I have a look at the existing page.

Cover Letter

Hi there, I understand your landing page isn't converting as well as you'd like. Here's an ebook landing page I wrote and designed: <link to page> - It was written specifically for 4K.com's target audience, aspiring 4K TV owners. My client was really impressed: "I honestly did not expect the excellent quality of work that they delivered. It was timely, professional and I did not have to give much direction... Excellent work and very happy with the results. I will be contracting her for more work. they went above and beyond." - Richard, co-founder at 4K.com

They addressed my needs in the first line. Gave me a relevant sample of their work and asked actual questions about the project. And guess what - it was the winning proposal at $90/h, which was above the average amount bid for the job.

The proposal probably didn't take them more than 20 minutes to write, but it ticked all the boxes I had as a client. It also shows that you CAN charge premium prices if you are good at what you do.

Client Retention

Client retention is the single biggest area that failing Upworkers overlook. It is 10x harder to sign a new client than it is to retain an existing one, so why do so many people never contact their clients again after they finish a job?

Guess what? If a client likes you and you did a good job, if you stay in touch with them they're more likely to rehire you. I personally try to follow up with my core clients at least every week. This can involves asking about performance, sending them useful advice for their project or even sending holiday greetings. It only takes a few minutes but it is invaluable to the amount of repeat work it will bring you. Once again, freelancing is a people business.

A personal example. My core Upwork business is writing sales copy for e-commerce products. In the past 6 months alone, I've gotten repeat business from these clients doing the following:

- Copy for an advertising flyer
- Email marketing
- PPC Campaign Analysis and Management
- Website copy

…and that's just some of the repeat work.

Could they have hired another freelancer who was more experienced to do this? You bet! But they didn't. Why? Because they'd already worked with me, knew I did good work that was delivered on time and most importantly of all...THEY LIKED ME!

Client retention is even more valuable than ever in 2017 after Upwork changed their fee structure. Now the first $500 of each client contract is subject to a 20% Upwork fee. After you've earned $500, the fee drops down to the standard 10%. If you're good enough to do more than $10,000 worth of work for a client - the fee lowers once again to just 5%.

Let's take a look at the numbers. Working for 1 client, or working for 10 clients for the same total amount. Let's see how much you actually take home after applying Upwork fees.

	Amount billed	Take Home Amount After Upwork Fees
Long Term Client	1500	1300
10 one-off clients	1500	1200

	Amount billed	Take Home Amount After Upwork Fees
Long Term Client	5000	4450

10 one-off clients   5000   4000

So for $5,000 of billed work - you take home almost $500 more from a long-term client than you do for multiple one-off clients. And that's ignoring all the extra work that it takes to find a new client in the first place.

How to retain over half your clients

So how do you make clients like you enough to give you repeat work - even in different fields than the initial project?

Step 1: Make sure the initial project goes off without a hitch

This sounds simple, but doing your first project well is so vital to getting repeat work. Submit your work on time (preferably before any deadline), put in the extra effort and show the client you care. If you nail the first project, you also get more leeway on future ones.

Clients are much more likely to accept minor errors on your 5th project together than your first.

Step 2: Follow up with clients after the project is finished

This step is also obvious yet it's another overlooked area.

Once you've submitted the work - check in with the client a few days or a week later to see how their project is going. Don't just say hello though - make the communication valuable.

For example - if you designed a logo for their website, go to the site and see if there is potential for more graphic design work.

Or for marketing people - if you just ran a successful Facebook campaign, ask them if they also use/plan to use Google adwords.

You don't need to pitch any additional work to them at this stage, just simply offer some useful and valuable advice or thoughts.

Step 3: Make yourself invaluable

Constantly go above and beyond for the client. This doesn't mean spending hours doing free work - just make sure you overdeliver on any project that you do.

If you can do that, then you become invaluable and the client won't be able to resist hiring you for future projects.

Step 3.5: Lose the battle, but win the war

Sometimes a client will offer you work that you know is not a good use of your time or their money. In these cases it's better to help them find a more cost-efficient method, and in turn free yourself up for more valuable work.

I once had a client ask me to do roughly 10 hours of data entry on a project, and he was willing to pay me $57/h to do so. This was neither a good use of my time nor his money. I suggested he find a cheaper freelancer to do the data entry (low skill work) so I could concentrate on things that would be more valuable to the project. This put me in great standing with him and resulted in much more work down the line.

Case Study: How I turned a $220 job into $9,000 worth of work

One of the very first jobs I won on Upwork was writing food blogs. My initial job was to write 5 blog posts for $220. Now I could have just done the initial work and moved on to another client, but I didn't.

After completing the job I did some further research on the client and saw their site had a huge number of posts on it, and there was room for a lot more. I decided to send them a number of potential blog topics that were in line with their current offerings. They liked a few of them and commissioned me to write another 10 articles. With around 15 minutes of research and brainstorming I'd already doubled my previous contract. This pattern continued for another 9 months in which I ended up doing $9,000 worth of work for one single site. As an added bonus here, the relief in knowing that you'll have recurring income from a client on a monthly basis is a huge asset.

Your rates and how to raise them

The default Upwork profile rate when you first sign up is $10/h, criminally low for anyone living in a first world country. But for some unknown reason, many Upwork freelancers start off at this rate. If you have zero experience and are a native English speaker I recommend starting out at $25/h, regardless of your field. There are cases of people starting out at $50/h or higher and succeeding.

The key to raising rates is to be as aggressive as possible. Too many freelancers spend way too much time in the lower rungs (<$30/h) before making the leap. My personal strategy is to raise my rates every time I win an hourly job at my previous rate.

So once you've landed a $25/h job, change your profile rate to $30/h. Once you sign a client at $30/h, change your profile rate to $35/h and so on. This way the higher rates come quicker than you think.

Another advantage of raising your hourly rate is that it allows you to bid more for fixed price jobs. If you're a web designer who only charges $20/h, it's hard to bid $1,500 to build a site for someone. But if you charge $50/h, that price becomes much more reasonable to a potential client.

Many people have a fear that clients will extensively study their previous rates, and then demand a big discount. As someone with over 4 years of experience, I can tell you that this doesn't happen. No one cares what you USED to charge for work, they only care about what you charge now.

One more note on rates. Experiment with ending your rates with a 7 or a 9 as opposed to a 5 or a 0 to stand out from the crowd. E.g. $37/h vs. $35/h - This is just a small tactic to help draw someone's eye to your profile/job bid instead of others.

Raising Your Rates With Existing Clients

It's hard to raise your rates with existing clients, and asking for a raise too early is a very easy way to lose a contract. If you are going to ask them, do so after you've been working together for at least 3 months and only ask for a raise of 20% or less. The reason for this is that in the client's mind your initial rate is the price they should pay for the work. So they are naturally reluctant to give you a large increase. You can save your big leaps for new clients.

Summary

And there you have it.

Making money online via freelancing on Upwork is easier than you think. For anyone who wants to quit their job, work for themselves and work from anywhere, this is the perfect way to do it.

I hope you will apply these lessons, and feel free to constantly refer back to this guide throughout your Upwork career. If you win just a single job using any of these tips then I've succeeded in my mission and your purchase will have been worth your money.

www.ingramcontent.com/pod-product-compliance
Lightning Source LLC
Chambersburg PA
CBHW030527220526
45463CB00007B/2747